HEATHCLIFF
GONE FISHIN'!

The funniest feline in America delights millions of fans every day as he appears in over 500 newspapers. You'll have a laugh a minute as Heathcliff tangles with the milkman, the fish store owner, the tuna fisherman and just about everyone else he runs into. If you're looking for some fun, look no farther. Heathcliff is here.

HEATHCLIFF®
GONE FISHIN'!

by George Gately

CHARTER BOOKS, NEW YORK

Cartoons previously published in
Wicked Loving Heathcliff

HEATHCLIFF GONE FISHIN'!

A Charter Book / published by arrangement with
McNaught Syndicate, Inc. and DIC Audiovisuel, Inc.

PRINTING HISTORY
Charter Original / June 1985

ISBN: 0-441-32231-X

Charter Books are published by The Berkley Publishing Group,
200 Madison Avenue, New York, New York 10016.
PRINTED IN THE UNITED STATES OF AMERICA

"ONE TOY MOUSE, GREY.... ONE BALL OF YARN,
YELLOW.... ONE FISH BONE..."

"...WHOOPEE CAT FOOD, UP THREE....ACE CAT FOOD, DOWN A HALF...MERRY MEW INC., NO CHANGE."

"HE FANCIES HIMSELF A COMEDIAN."

"HE'S BEEN SAVING UP FOR A HERRING."

"YOU DON'T HAVE TO MEASURE EVERY DIVOT!"

"GRANDMA, HAVE YOU SEEN MY BADMINTON SET?"

"YOUR DOG FOOD SECTION IS TWO FEET LONGER THAN YOUR CAT FOOD SECTION."

"WILL YOU JUST LET ME HOLLER 'FORE'?!"

"IT'S NICE THAT THE YOUNGSTERS
GET ALONG SO WELL!"

"IT'S GOOD YOU WORE
YOUR HARD HAT!"

"IT'S ON THEIR LIST!...THEY ORDERED
CHOCOLATE MILK!"

"... AND HIS 'TUFFO' WATCH IS STILL TICKING!"

"IT'S ELVIS PRESLEY NIGHT!"

"I'M GLAD *SOMEBODY* IS GOING TO
RING IN THE NEW YEAR!"

"SOMEONE'S HERE TO SEE YOU... OR IS THAT
WHY YOU LEFT IN THE FIRST PLACE?"

"NOW HE'S TEACHING NIGHT SCHOOL!"

"I'LL HANDLE THIS!"

"YOU TOO ?"

"IT'S A POSTER FOR YOU FROM CRAZY SHIRLEY."

"IT'S A GOOD THING WE'RE GOING OUT TONIGHT!"

"HE ENJOYS AN EGGNOG DURING THE HOLIDAYS!"

"IS YOUR DAD STAYING WITH US RIGHT THROUGH THE HOLIDAYS?"

"IT'S SO HARD TO KEEP HIM TUCKED IN!"

"END OF THE YEAR INVENTORY?"

"NEVER STAND UNDER THE MISTLETOE
WHEN CHAUNCY IS AROUND!"

"HE'LL DUMP THAT ON THE EXACT STROKE OF MIDNIGHT."

"HAPPY NEW YEAR, RUDY."

"WHAT?...LOST YOUR MITTEN?...YOU NAUGHTY KITTEN!"

"IT'S A BRAND NEW CAT FOOD....CHINESE STYLE."

"RIGHT IN HERE...THEY'RE WAITING FOR YOU!"

"THIS IS THE EXPRESS LANE!"

"WE HAVEN'T BEEN DUMPING OVER ANY
GARBAGE CANS, HAVE WE?"

"I KNOW HE'S GOING TO DUMP IT, SO I FIGURED
I MIGHT AS WELL GIFT WRAP IT!"

"HE CHECKS EVERYWHERE FOR MICE."

"NEVER MIND THE SUGGESTIONS!"

"I'M NOT MAKING A MOVE UNTIL I FIND OUT
WHAT TRICK YOU'VE GOT UP YOUR SLEEVE!"

"I TOLD MY SECRETARY I REFUSE TO SEE YOU!"

"HE RAISES THE BATON....."

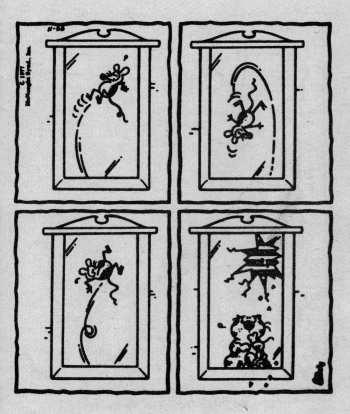

"HERE'S ANOTHER ONE YOU CAN OPEN EARLY."

"ARE YOU PLANNING ANY THANKSGIVING FESTIVITIES?"

"I GET THE OTHER DRUMSTICK, IF YOU DON'T MIND!"

"HE'S GOT HIS OWN RECIPE FOR TURKEY LEFTOVERS!"

"I MADE OUT A GIFT LIST, SO THAT
WE DON'T FORGET ANYBODY."

"YES!...YOU'RE ON IT!"

"I'M MISSING AN EEL!"

"HE'S EXPECTING A COLD WINTER."

"MAY I SUGGEST A NEW YEAR'S RESOLUTION?"

"ENJOY YOUR DINNER?"

"HERE COMES GREAT, BIG, LOVABLE CHAUNCY!"

"I THINK HE'S HELPING GRANDMA WITH HER GIRDLE."

"I'D LIKE TO HAVE HIS BLUE BOOTIES BRONZED."

"ATTA BOY!... IT'S STARTING TO MOVE!"

"NET ?... I DON'T USE A NET."

"THEY COME FROM MILES AROUND TO SEE THE GURU!"

"GOOD WORK, BOYS!... YOU FINALLY TREED HIM!"

"I ASSUME THIS IS YOUR BOOKMARK!"

"IT'S A FLOUNDER WITH A FILE IN IT!"

"LOOK OUT, RALPH!...YOU'RE APPROACHING
'DEAD MAN'S CURVE'!"

"GOOD MORNING, HEATHCLIFF."

"REPEAT AFTER ME..."THE DOGCATCHERS OATH"..."

♪ "WHOOPEE CAT FOOD' CAN'T BE BEAT...
...BUY SOME FOR A KITTY TREAT!" ♪

"HEATHCLIFF!....
SUPPERTIME!"

"AND HERE WE SIT IN A GAS LINE!"

"IT'S JUST WHAT YOU NEED.....
         'THE GARBAGE DUMPER'S DIET'!"

"THOSE ARE HIS VERY FIRST MUG SHOTS."

"WOULD YOU PREFER FISH ALMONDINE, OR FISH VERONIQUE, OR FISH A LA FLORENTINE, OR FISH NEWBURG, OR...."

"YOU AND YOUR FRIEND CAN JUST MARCH
RIGHT OUT OF HERE!"

"DUE TO THE HEAVY SNOWFALL, THE FOLLOWING SCHOOLS WILL BE CLOSED FOR TODAY...."

"I'LL BET YOU FORGOT TO BATHE THE CAT AGAIN!"

"DARN !...AND I TIED A STRING ON MY FINGER!"

"SOMEONE TURNED YOUR TROMBONE
INTO A PLANTER."

"DIDUMS MOMMIE'S BOY GETTUM HIS EXERCISE?"

"IT'S A RICH, HEAVY CREAM, WITH A CAT-PROOF CAP."

" YOU SEE BEFORE YOU ... A SINNER ...."

"WHAT'S YOUR DOG HOUSE DOING IN THE MIDDLE OF THE ROAD ?!"

"HIS DAD SENT HIM A GIFT...A LICENSE PLATE."

"WELL, THEY CERTAINLY CAN'T BE ACCUSED OF TYPE CASTING!"

"ARE YOU TRYING TO START SOMETHING ?!"

"READY GANG?...HERE COME THE ORNAMENTS!"

"TONIGHT, WE WELCOME OUR NEWEST MEMBER TO 'GARBAGE DUMPERS ANONYMOUS.'"

"I FOUND YOUR COLORING FOR THE EASTER EGGS!"

"HE'S DOING 'A PARTRIDGE IN A PEAR TREE'!"

"THIS IS NO DAY TO PICK ON AN IRISH WOLFHOUND!"

"YOU'LL LEAVE YOUR BOOTH GRAY
LIKE EVERYONE ELSE!"

"I TELL YOU, J.R., THERE WOULDN'T BE
ANOTHER T.V. SERIES LIKE IT!"

"MY GOSH!...THE BEACH IS MOBBED TODAY!"

"CASING THE JOINT ?!"

"I'M HELPING HIM WITH HIS LAST MINUTE SHOPPING."

"IT WAS A SPLIT...WE LOST AND HEATHCLIFF WON!"

"HEATHCLIFF TOOK A STOCKING OFF MY CLOTHESLINE!"

"OH GOOD!...YOU FOUND MY GLASSES!"

"IT'S ONE OF HIS BUSIER DAYS."

"HE EATS MORE THAN *YOUR* BOYFRIEND!"

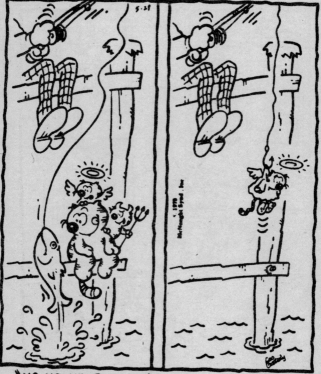

"NO, NO, HEATHCLIFF!"
"G'WAN, GRAB IT!"

"WE'VE GOT SOME PRETTY HIGH-CLASS MICE!"

"DON'T ASK US, HEATHCLIFF...WE DON'T KNOW ANYTHING ABOUT THE BIRDS AND THE BEES."

"LOOKS LIKE WE'RE SHIPPING OUT!"

"...AND NOW A REQUEST FOR HEATHCLIFF NUTMEG
AND ALL YOU JIVE CATS OUT THERE...."